Twelve Little Ducks

Written by Brian Birchall
Photographs by Jan McPherson

Twelve little ducks come down to the river.
They are looking for bugs and plants
and tiny things to eat.

They look down into puddles
and they push their beaks under stones.

Heads down, bottoms up,
splashing through the water –
twelve little ducks looking like stones.

Quack! Quack! Quack!
They follow their mother into the deep river
and race across the water
like little speedboats.

They splash and dive, feed and swim, all afternoon.

Quack! Quack!
Twelve little ducks come out of the water
to dry on the warm stones.

Quack!
Twelve little ducks
are creeping close to their mother.

Quack!
Twelve little ducks are safe and warm
. . . and asleep.

THE
HIGHGATE
COLLECTION

United States edition published in 1991 by
Steck-Vaughn Company
P.O. Box 26015
Austin, Texas 78755.
Steck-Vaughn Company is a subsidiary
of National Education Corporation.

First published in 1989 in New Zealand by
Nelson Price Milburn Ltd.
1 Te Puni Street, Petone

Twelve Little Ducks
ISBN   0 8114 2692 0
Text © Brian Birchall
Photographs © Jan McPherson
© 1990 Nelson Price Milburn Ltd.

Printed in Hong Kong.

Library of Congress Cataloging-in-Publication Data: Birchall, Brian, 1932– / Twelve little ducks /
written by Brian Birchall; photographs by Jan McPherson.
p. cm. SUMMARY: Text and pictures depict twelve little ducks feeding and playing in the river and
later sleeping near their mother, safe and warm.
ISBN 0-8114-2692-0
1. Ducks — Juvenile literature. [1. Ducks.] I. McPherson, Jan, ill. II Title. QL696.A52852 1990
598.4`1—dc20   90–10054   CIP   AC

ABE-7562